Soccer Mom COOKBOOK

McClanahan
Publishing House

International Standard Book Number 0-913383 59 7
Library of Congress Catalog Card Number 98-84810

Cover design, illustrations and book layout by James Asher Graphics
Editorial Assistants: Luke Cunningham, Derek McQuigg and Austin Gresham
Recipes by Lyon County, Kentucky soccer fans

Manufactured in the United States of America
For use of this cookbook as a fundraiser activity call for group rates.
All individual book order correspondence should be addressed to:

McClanahan Publishing House, Inc.
P. O. Box 100
Kuttawa, KY 42055
1-800-544-6959
email: kybooks@apex.net
www.kybooks.com

Introduction

For the moms of soccer players everywhere, this cookbook is dedicated to you! We hope that in using these recipes your life will be made a little less stressful as you try to juggle your "mom" activities along with your professional roles.

In this book we have compiled recipes straight from the files of everyday mothers who wish to provide tasty meals for their family. Most are one dish meals and a few recipes sprinkled in for breads, salads, sides and desserts. All are easy to prepare and foods loved by everyone.

A special thanks to Dr. Debra Wilder for her tidbits of sports/health tips scattered throughout the book. A helpful glossary of soccer terms is also included.

"Hats off" to all moms racing to meet those practice schedules and games. We hope you enjoy our *Soccer Mom Cookbook.*

High Performance
Pesto Ravioli with Chicken

2 teaspoons olive oil
2 chicken breasts, sliced
3/4 cup chicken broth
9-ounce package frozen cheese filled ravioli
3 small zucchini, sliced
1 large red bell pepper, sliced
1/4 cup refrigerated pesto
Parmesan cheese to garnish

Heat oil in skillet. Cook chicken until brown. Remove chicken; add broth and ravioli to skillet. Bring to a boil, cover and simmer 4 minutes until ravioli is tender. Stir in zucchini, pepper and chicken. Cook 3 minutes; stir in pesto and sprinkle with cheese.

Scorer's
South of the Border Casserole

8 corn tortillas
3 tablespoons salad oil
1 pound ground chuck
1 medium onion, diced
1 small garlic clove, minced
Two 15-ounce cans refried beans
28-ounce can whole peeled tomatoes,
    chopped
6-ounce can tomato paste
1-ounce can chopped chili peppers
2 teaspoons sugar
1 teaspoon salt
1/2 teaspoon oregano
1/4 teaspoon pepper
1 to 2 cups grated sharp cheddar cheese

In a 12-inch skillet, fry tortillas in hot salad oil for a few seconds. Remove to paper towels and cut into 1/2-inch strips. Using same skillet, over medium heat, brown ground chuck with garlic and onion; remove from heat and drain. Stir in beans, tomatoes, tomato paste, chili peppers, sugar, salt, oregano and pepper. Preheat oven to 350°. In a 9x13-inch baking dish arrange 1/3 of beef mixture, top with 1/3 of the tortilla strips. Repeat layering ending with tortilla strips on top. Sprinkle cheese on top. Bake 30 minutes or until hot.

This is a meal with salad and hot bread.

Makes 12 servings

Countdown
Chicken and Noodle Casserole

5 to 6 chicken breasts, cooked and deboned
4 to 5 green onions
2 tablespoons butter
12 ounces fettuccini
Fresh grated Parmesan cheese

Sauce

1 cup mayonnaise
1 cup sour cream
1 can cream of mushroom soup
1 1/2 teaspoon Dijon mustard
3 tablespoons dry sherry
6 ounces medium sharp cheddar cheese

Sautè onions in green onions in butter. Cook noodles according to package directions. Combine chicken and onions. In a separate bowl mix sauce ingredients. Place noodles in 9x13-inch casserole dish. Cover with chicken and onion. Top with sauce and sprinkle with Parmesan. Bake at 350° for 35 minutes or until top is light brown.

Hand Ball Burritos

1 pound ground beef
1 can chili beans
1 package taco seasoning mix
1/2 can jalapeño relish
Large flour tortilla shells
Velveeta Cheese, grated

Brown and drain meat. Mash beans and stir into meat. Add taco seasoning and relish; mix well. Spoon onto tortillas; add cheese and wrap. Place on cookie sheet and bake at 400° for 15 minutes.

Dr. Deb's Advice

For pregame meals try to select foods that are high in carbohydrate and low in fat.

Stadium Club Strawberry Pizza

1 roll sugar cookie dough,
    at room temperature
2 cups powdered sugar
8-ounce package cream cheese
8-ounce carton whipped topping
1 quart strawberries
1 package strawberry glaze

Spray a 9x13-inch baking dish with cooking spray. Press cookie dough evenly into dish; bake for 10 to 15 minutes at 350°. Let cool completely. Mix powdered sugar, cream cheese and whipped topping with electric mixer. Top cooled crust with cream cheese mixture. Mix strawberries and glaze together. Pour over cream cheese mixture. Chill for 2 hours before serving.

Serves 8 to 12

Crossbar
Barbecue Pork and Beans

2 pounds lean pork meat, cut into chunks
1/2 cup chopped green pepper
1/2 cup chopped onion
One 16-ounce bottle barbecue sauce
Two 16-ounce cans baked beans, drained

Spray crock pot with cooking spray. Mix meat, green pepper, onions and 1/2 of the barbecue sauce together in crock pot. Cook on high for 4 to 6 hours or on low for 8 to 10 hours. When the meat is tender, stir in remaining barbecue sauce and drained baked beans. Serve with salad and corn bread.

Serves 4

Soccer Ball Beef Stroganoff

1/2 cup minced onion
1 clove garlic, minced
1/4 cup butter
1 pound sirloin, cut in strips
1 tablespoon flour
1 teaspoon salt
1/4 teaspoon Accent
1/4 teaspoon paprika
8 ounces fresh mushrooms, sliced
1/4 cup red wine
1 can cream of chicken soup
1 cup sour cream
Parsley or chives to garnish

Sautè onion and garlic in butter. Stir in sirloin and brown. Stir in flour, spices and mushrooms; cook 5 minutes. Add wine and soup; cook 10 minutes. Stir in sour cream; heat thoroughly and serve over noodles. Garnish with parsley or chives.

Crowd Pleasing White Chili

2 to 3 large cans white northern beans
6 chicken breasts,
   cooked and shredded or chopped
Broth from chicken
2 onions, chopped
4 cloves garlic
Chili powder to taste
   or one package chili seasoning
1 to 2 cans cream of mushroom soup

Put all ingredients in crock pot and cook on low as long as desired. When serving top with salsa and sour cream.

Goal Bound Beef Casserole

1 pound ground beef
1 1/2 teaspoons salt
1 large onion, chopped
1/2 green pepper, chopped
1/2 pound cheese, grated
1 cup elbow macaroni
1 pint tomatoes
1 teaspoon prepared mustard
1 small can mushrooms
   or 1 can mushroom soup

Cook meat, salt, onion and green pepper until meat is brown. Cook macaroni until almost tender, about 5 minutes. Mix all ingredients in casserole and bake at 350° about 1 hour.

Corner Pass Crock Pot Steak

One 10 1/2-ounce can
   cream of mushroom soup, undiluted
One 10 1/2-ounce can onion soup,
   undiluted
Round steak, cut up and rolled in flour

Put soups in crock pot. Add steak; cook on low for 6 to 8 hours.

Dr. Deb's Advice

Drink at least one glass of water for every hour before games. This will help to prevent cramps.

Microwave Post-game Potato Delight

1/4 cup butter
1 1/2 teaspoon salt
1/4 teaspoon pepper
4 medium potatoes, washed,
    unpeeled and cut into 1/8-inch slices
1/2 cup green pepper,
    cut into 1/4-inch strips
1/2 cup onion, sliced

In a 8x12-inch baking dish, melt butter on high. Stir in salt and pepper. Stir in remaining ingredients until coated with butter. Cover, cook on high, stirring every two minutes, until potatoes are fork tender or about 15 minutes. Let stand 15 minutes.

Trophy Chicken Tetrazzini

3/4 cup butter
3/4 cup flour
4 cups chicken broth
3 cups half and half
1/2 cup dry sherry
1/4 teaspoon nutmeg
3/4 teaspoon pepper
2 teaspoons salt
1/2 teaspoon garlic salt
1 pound thin spaghetti cooked al dente,
   drained
6 cups diced, cooked chicken
4-ounce can sliced mushrooms, drained
1 1/2 cups grated Parmesan cheese
Paprika

Melt butter, add flour and cook a minute. Add chicken broth, cream, sherry and seasonings; cook until thick, smooth and bubbly. Add more broth or cream if too thick. Grease two large flat baking dishes. In each dish layer as follows: a fourth of the spaghetti, a fourth of the chicken, one half of the mushrooms, one fourth of the sauce, one fourth of the spaghetti, one fourth of the chicken, one fourth of the sauce and half of the cheese. Sprinkle tops lightly with paprika. Bake at 350° for 30 to 40 minutes. If made ahead and refrigerated, bake longer. It should be very hot and bubbly when serving.

Serves 12

Hall of Fame Frozen Cherry Salad

9 ounces whipped topping
1 can sweetened condensed milk
1 can cherry pie mix
8 ounces crushed pineapple, saving juice
1/2 cup nuts, chopped

Beat whipped topping and milk together. Fold in cherry pie mix, pineapple and nuts. Pour into dish and freeze. Cut into squares to serve.

Hamburger Goulash for Halfbacks

1 pound ground chuck
1 cup cooked minute rice
8-ounce can tomato sauce
Minced dried onions to taste
Salt to taste
4 slices American cheese

Brown meat and drain. Add remaining ingredients except cheese. Bring to a boil then simmer for 15 minutes. Top with cheese; serve when cheese is bubbly.

Serves 4

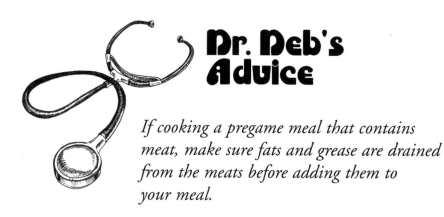

Dr. Deb's Advice

If cooking a pregame meal that contains meat, make sure fats and grease are drained from the meats before adding them to your meal.

Free Kick French Bread

One loaf French bread, unsliced
8 ounces sliced Swiss, American
    or mozzarella cheese
1/2 cup margarine or butter, melted
2 to 3 tablespoons sesame or poppy seed

Heat oven to 375°. Slice bread into 1-inch slices, cutting to but not through bottom of loaf. Place loaf on sheet of heavy-duty foil. Cut cheese into triangles; place between bread slices. Drizzle margarine and sprinkle with seed between and over bread; do not seal. Bake for 10 to 12 minutes.

May also be placed on grill.

Makes 16 slices

Keeper Cavatina

1 pound ground beef
1/2 medium onion, chopped
1 large jar spaghetti sauce
1 can sliced mushrooms
1/2 teaspoon Italian seasoning
1/2 box of corkscrew noodles, cooked
1/2 package sliced pepperoni
1 package grated mozzarella cheese

Brown ground beef and onion; drain. Mix in remaining ingredients except cheese. Place half of mixture in 9x12-inch casserole dish. Layer with half the mozzarella cheese. Top with remaining mixture and bake at 350° for 20 minutes. Remove from oven and layer with remaining cheese. Return to oven until cheese is melted.

Halfback Hamburger Pie

1 pound ground beef
1/2 cup chopped onion
One 16-ounce can cut green beans, drained
One 10 3/4-ounce can
    condensed tomato soup
1/4 cup water
3/4 teaspoon salt
1/8 teaspoon pepper
3 medium potatoes, peeled and quartered
1 beaten egg
Milk
Salt and pepper to taste
1/2 cup shredded American cheese

Preheat oven to 350°. In a large skillet cook ground beef and onion until meat is browned and onion is tender; drain off fat. Stir in beans, soup, water, salt and pepper. Pour mixture into a 1 1/2-quart baking dish. Cook potatoes in a covered pan in boiling salted water about 20 minutes or until tender; drain. Mash while hot; stir in enough egg and enough milk to make potatoes fluffy yet stiff enough to hold their shape. Season with salt and pepper. Drop potatoes in mounds atop meat mixture. Sprinkle with cheese. Bake, uncovered, for 25 to 30 minutes or until heated through.

Makes 4 to 6 servings

Chicken Lickin' Casserole

6 large chicken breasts
3 cans asparagus
1 medium onion, chopped
1 can mushroom pieces
1/2 cup butter
2 cans cream of chicken soup
1/2 pound cheddar cheese
1 teaspoon salt
1/2 teaspoon white pepper
1 teaspoon Accent
1 small jar pimentos, chopped
3/4 can evaporated milk
1/4 tablespoons hot sauce
1 tablespoons soy sauce

Boil chicken, debone and chop. Cover bottom of large dish or 2 medium dishes with asparagus. Layer chicken over asparagus. Sautè onion and mushrooms in butter; add remaining ingredients and simmer until cheese melts. Pour mixture over chicken and asparagus. Top with slivered almonds, if desired. Bake, uncovered, in 350° oven until bubbly.

Serves 10

The Better Team's Fruit Salad

1 can peach pie filling
1 package frozen strawberries, thawed
1 large can pineapple chunks, drained
1 medium can mandarin oranges, drained
2 bananas, sliced
2 cups white seedless grapes

Mix all ingredients together and serve over a bed of lettuce.

Penalty Pasta Salad

1 package colored spiral pasta,
   cooked and drained
1/2 head cauliflower, cut in bite-size pieces
1/2 medium onion, chopped
1 head broccoli, cut in bite-size pieces
1/2 green pepper, chopped
1 bottle Ranch or creamy Italian dressing

Toss all ingredients and let sit for 45 minutes to 1 hour before serving.

Why not add shrimp for a change?

Forward's Fudge Cake

1 package chocolate pudding and pie filling
1 box chocolate cake mix
1 cup chocolate chips
1/2 cup chopped nuts

Cook chocolate pudding and pie filling as directed on package. Blend dry cake mix into hot pudding. Pour into greased 9x13-inch pan. Sprinkle chocolate chips and nuts on top. Bake at 350 ° for 30 to 35 minutes. Serve warm with whipped cream.

Fettuccini for Forwards

12 ounces fettuccini
4 tablespoons butter
3/4 cup grated Parmesan cheese
1/2 cup heavy whipping cream

Cook fettuccini in boiling water until tender. In saucepan melt butter; add cheese and cream. Beat together with wire whisk. Drain fettuccini and add to cheese mixture.

Dr. Deb's Advice

If a cramp occurs continue to drink water even if you are not thirsty.

Super Soccer Nachos

1 pound ground chuck or turkey
1 package taco seasoning
1 bag tortilla chips
8 ounces shredded cheddar cheese

Prepare taco meat mixture using directions on taco seasoning package. Line a shallow glass baking dish with chips. Cover chips with meat mixture and cheese. Microwave for 1 minute or until cheese melts.

PK Pork Chop Supper

2 tablespoons shortening
4 pork chops, 1/2-inch thick
1 teaspoon salt
Dash of pepper
1/2 cup chicken broth
4 small potatoes, peeled and halved
    or quartered
4 medium carrots, peeled and cut up
1 small onion, chopped
2 tablespoons flour
1/4 cup cold water

Heat shortening in 4-quart pressure cooker. Season chops with salt and pepper. Brown on both sides in hot shortening. Add broth; place vegetables on top of chops. Sprinkle with additional salt and pepper, if desired. Close cover securely; cook 10 minutes at 15 pounds pressure. Cool quickly under cold running water. Remove chops and vegetables to serving dish. Blend flour and cold water. Add to juices in pan; cook and stir until thick and bubbly.

Serves 4

Kickoff Cobbler

1/2 stick margarine
29-ounce can sliced peaches
1/2 cup sugar
1/2 cup milk
1/2 cup self-rising flour

Melt margarine in a saucepan; add peaches. Pour peaches and margarine in an 8x8x2-inch baking dish. Mix sugar, milk and flour and pour over peaches. Bake for 25 to 30 minutes in a 350° oven.

Pele's Sole

1 1/2 pounds sole or other fish fillet
Salt and pepper
1/2 cup mayonnaise
1/2 cup shredded cheese
1 egg white
Dash of cayenne

Place fish fillets on broiler rack and sprinkle with salt and pepper. Broil about 4 inches from heat for 10 minutes, depending on thickness of fillet. Combine mayonnaise, cheese and cayenne. Beat egg white until stiff and fold into dressing. Spread on fish and broil until puffed and lightly browned. Serve immediately. Crappie is a great substitute.

Serves 4

Hot Stuff Hash Brown Casserole

32-ounce bag frozen hash browns
   or tater tots
1 can cream of celery soup
1 cup cheese, shredded
Corn flake crumbs
1 stick butter

Thaw hash browns. Mix all ingredients except butter and crumbs. Pour mixture into oblong casserole dish; sprinkle with crumbs and pour melted butter over top. Bake at 350° for 30 to 40 minutes.

Keeper's Choice Chili

2 to 3 pounds ground chuck
28-ounce can pork and beans
40-ounce can tomato juice
1 package mild chili seasoning mix

Brown meat in a large pot; drain fat. Add remaining ingredients and simmer until thickened. Great over hot dogs with relish.

Concession Stand Green Tomato Relish

10 large green tomatoes
1/2 cup salt
4 cups onions
10 green sweet peppers
1 medium head cabbage
1 hot pepper
6 cups sugar
1 tablespoon celery seed
2 tablespoons mustard seed
4 cups vinegar
2 cups water

Grind tomatoes; add salt. Let set overnight and drain. Next day bring remaining ingredients to a boil; add vegetables. Simmer 3 minutes and fill sterilized jars using sterilized seals.

Great served on grilled hot dogs!

Linesman's German Chocolate Cake

1 box white cake mix
4 1/2-ounce package
   instant chocolate pudding mix
2 cups milk
2 eggs

Combine cake mix and chocolate pudding mix. Add milk and eggs; beat well with mixer. Pour into two greased and floured 8 or 9-inch layer pans. Bake at 350° for 35 to 40 minutes or until done when tested. When cool frost with Coconut Pecan Frosting.

Coconut Pecan Frosting

1 cup evaporated milk
1/2 pound margarine
3 egg yolks
1 teaspoon vanilla
1 cup sugar
1 can coconut
1 cup chopped pecans

Cook milk, margarine, egg yolks, vanilla and sugar over medium heat. Stir constantly until mixture thickens, about 12 minutes. Add coconut and pecans.

Dr. Deb's Advice

If a head injury occurs during practice or game only drink fluids after the accident has occurred. Do not eat anything for at least a few hours after the game or practice.

Soccer Field Swiss Bliss

2 pounds round steak, cut 1-inch thick
1 tablespoon butter
1 envelope dry onion soup mix
1/2 cup bell pepper, chopped
1 pound can tomatoes, drained, reserving juice
1 can mushroom soup
1/4 teaspoon salt
1 tablespoon steak sauce
1 tablespoon cornstarch

Line a 9x13-inch casserole dish with foil. Place steak in pan and add butter, onion soup, bell pepper and drained tomatoes to the steak. Shake together in a jar, mushroom soup, salt, tomato juice, steak sauce and cornstarch. Pour over steak. Close foil and bake 2 hours at 250°.

Eat Your Vegetables Casserole

2 cans mixed vegetables, drained
1 jar cheese or small box Velveeta
1 stick butter, cut in half
Butter crackers, crushed

Mix vegetables, melted cheese and 1/2 the butter. Put in a casserole dish. Sprinkle crackers on top; pour rest of butter over. Cook at 350° for about 20 minutes or until crackers are starting to brown.

Great way to get kids to eat their vegetables.

Center Circle Chicken-n-Rice

1 whole chicken or 2 to 3 cans
    deboned chicken or turkey
2 cups brown or white rice
10 1/2-ounce can cream of mushroom soup
10 1/2-ounce can cream of chicken soup
Salt, pepper and poultry seasoning to taste

Boil or pressure cook chicken. With leftover chicken broth prepare rice according to package directions. If using canned chicken or turkey, prepare rice with water. Mix all ingredients and pour into 9x13-inch baking dish. Bake for 30 to 60 minutes at 350°.

Serves 6 to 8

Red Card Red Beans & Rice

2 cans red kidney beans
1 can water
1 package Polska Kielbasa, cut in slices
Chopped green pepper and onion to taste
Salt and pepper to taste

Mix all ingredients in saucepan and cook about 20 to 30 minutes. Serve over white rice.

Serves 6

Dr. Deb's Advice

Pregame meals should never include fried foods.

Easy Stew for Strikers

3 pounds stew meat
1 onion, chopped
3 carrots, peeled and cut in 1-inch pieces
3 celery stalks, cut in 1-inch pieces
2 tablespoons instant beef bouillon
1/4 teaspoon seasoned salt
Ground pepper
3 tablespoons tapioca
8-ounce can tomato sauce
1/2 can water or wine

Put meat in baking dish. Layer vegetables on top. Sprinkle with dry ingredients; pour sauce and water on top. Cover and place in 350° oven for 45 minutes. Reduce heat to 250° and cook about 4 hours more. Serve with noodles, rice or mashed potatoes.

Pot roast or short ribs can be substituted for stew meat.

Major League
Mexican Corn Bread

1 1/2 cups self-rising cornmeal
1 cup milk
2 eggs
1/2 cup vegetable oil
One 8-ounce can cream style corn
1 medium onion, chopped
1/4 medium green pepper, chopped
1/2 cup shredded cheddar cheese

Preheat oven to 350°. Heat cast iron skillet with bottom covered with oil. Mix all ingredients except cheese. Pour half of mixture into hot skillet. Sprinkle with half of the shredded cheese. Repeat with other half of mixture and top with cheese. Bake at 350° for 45 minutes.

Penalty Kick Pot Pie

1 cup leftover, cooked and cut up meat,
    chicken, ham or turkey
2 cups or 1/2 bag frozen mixed vegetables
One 14 1/2-ounce can cream of mushroom,
    chicken or celery soup
Salt and pepper to taste
1 cup baking mix
1/2 cup milk
1 egg

Preheat oven to 400°. Spray a 9-inch pie dish with cooking spray. Mix meat with vegetables, soup and salt and pepper to taste. Add baking mix, milk and egg. Pour into pie dish. Bake for 30 minutes or until golden brown. Serve with salad.

Serves 4

Scorer's Super Soccer Snowballs

1/2 cup butter
1/2 cup flour
1 teaspoon vanilla
2 tablespoons powdered sugar
2 tablespoons water
Pinch of salt
Pecan halves
Powdered sugar for coating

Mix all ingredients except pecans and powdered sugar in a large bowl. Work until dough can be handled; may take a little more flour. Pinch off enough dough to cover a pecan half. Place on cookie sheet and bake at 300° for 30 minutes. Coat in powdered sugar when cool. Keep in refrigerator.

Makes 2 dozen

Passback Pot Roast

Beef Roast
2 tablespoons oil
Salt and pepper to taste
1/2 cup chopped onion
14 1/2-ounce can cream of mushroom soup
1/2 cup water
6 potatoes
6 carrots

Brown roast in oil in a skillet. Put in crock pot. Salt and pepper. Put onions on top of roast. Mix soup with water and pour over roast. Peel and cut up potatoes and carrots. Boil them in water until tender. Put in cool water and store in refrigerator. Cook roast in crock pot all day. About an hour before serving, put drained carrots and potatoes in crock pot to heat.

Training Taco Salad

2 pounds ground beef
1 package taco seasoning mix
1 head lettuce
1 large onion, chopped
1 large ripe tomato, chopped
1 package shredded mozzarella
  or cheddar cheese
1 large bag tortilla chips, crumbled
1 large bottle Thousand Island dressing

Brown ground beef; drain. Mix with seasoning, cool and set aside. Break lettuce into bite size pieces. In a large bowl, for the first layer, place lettuce; second layer - onion and tomato; third layer - ground beef; last layer - cheese, tortilla chips and dressing. The last layer should not be put on salad until ready to serve.

Serves 4 to 6

Tournament Hamburger Casserole

1 1/2 pounds ground beef
1 cup chopped onions, browned and drained
1 can corn, drained
1 can red beans, drained
1 can cream of mushroom soup
1 can cream of chicken soup
One 8-ounce carton sour cream
1 can pimentos
Salt and pepper to taste
3 cups flat noodles, cooked and drained

Mix all together and put in greased baking dish. Top with buttered bread crumbs; bake 30 minutes at 325°.

Brazilian Baked Potatoes and Chicken

1 cup cornmeal
2 tablespoons Italian seasoning mix
Salt and pepper to taste
1 1/2 to 2-pound cut-up fryer chicken
2/3 cup Dijon mustard
3 large potatoes, cut into pieces
1/2 tablespoon chili powder
Salt and pepper to taste
1 tablespoon olive oil

Spray one large baking sheet with cooking spray. Preheat oven and baking sheet to 450°. In large plastic bag, mix cornmeal, Italian seasoning, salt and pepper. Brush chicken with mustard and place in bag one piece at a time. Shake well to cover chicken. Place on baking sheet. In a separate plastic bag, combine potatoes, chili powder, salt, pepper and oil. Shake to coat the potatoes. Place on baking sheet with chicken. Bake 30 to 35 minutes, turning chicken once halfway through cooking.

Field Crock Pot Chicken

1 bottle barbecue sauce
1 teaspoon vegetable oil
Salt and pepper to taste
6 to 8 chicken breasts

Pour barbecue sauce in crock pot; stir in vegetable oil, salt and pepper. Add chicken, making sure they are coated well with sauce. Cook on low 8 hours and serve. Pork chops are also great to use.

Dr. Deb's Advice

To gain weight, properly choose foods with high amounts of protein and calories. Physical activities must increase even while trying to gain weight.

Midfielder Mick's
Macaroni and Cheese

1 cup elbow macaroni, uncooked
1 cup water
1 cup milk
2 tablespoons margarine
3 tablespoons flour
1 teaspoon salt
1 cup soft cheese, cubed

Combine ingredients, except cheese, in 2 1/2-quart casserole dish. Cover; microwave at high 4 1/2 minutes; stir. Cook at high 4 1/2 minutes more or until macaroni is tender. Add cheese; stir. Cover and allow to sit about 5 minutes. Stir and serve.

Sideline Brunch Casserole

1 pound pork sausage
6 eggs, slightly beaten
2 cups milk
1 teaspoon salt
1 teaspoon dry mustard
1 tablespoon Worcestershire sauce
4 tablespoons onion, chopped
4 tablespoons green pepper, chopped
2 slices day old bread, crushed
1 cup cheddar cheese, grated

Brown sausage; drain well and crumble. Mix with remaining ingredients and pour into 11x17-inch pan. Bake at 350° for 45 minutes.

Serves 6

Orange Smoothie

6 ounces frozen orange juice concentrate,
   unsweetened
1 cup milk
1 cup water
1 teaspoon vanilla
10 ice cubes

Place all ingredients in a blender. Fresh fruit, such as strawberries or peaches, can be added.

Half Volley Ham and Cheese Pie

8-ounce can crescent rolls
1 1/2 cups finely chopped ham
8-ounce package Monterey jack cheese
2 tablespoons Parmesan cheese
2 tablespoons chopped onion
2 eggs, beaten

Fit 5 triangles of crescent rolls in a pie dish. Combine remaining ingredients and pour over crescent rolls. Cut remaining triangles and arrange over mixture. May make ahead and refrigerate. Bake at 325° for 60 minutes.

Easy Score Mexicali Dinner

1 pound ground beef
1/2 cup chopped onion
6 ounces medium noodles, cooked and drained
16-ounce can tomatoes
6-ounce can tomato paste
6 ounces sharp process American cheese,
    shredded
1/2 cup sliced ripe olives
1 teaspoon salt
1/4 teaspoon dried basil, crushed
1/8 teaspoon pepper

Cook meat and onion in large skillet until onion is tender. Stir in noodles, tomatoes, tomato paste, 1 cup shredded cheese, olives and seasonings; turn into 2-quart casserole dish. Top with remaining cheese. Bake at 350° for 45 minutes.

Serves 6

Qualifying One Dish Meat and Potatoes

1 pound ground beef
1 can cream of celery soup
1 bag tater tots
1 bag cheddar cheese, grated
1 small onion, chopped

Cook ground beef; drain. Mix cream of celery, tater tots, onion and ground beef. Place in baking dish and top with cheese. Bake at 350° for 35 to 45 minutes.

Diving Save Dinner Rolls

1 can beer
2 teaspoons sugar
4 cups biscuit mix

Mix all ingredients; beat vigorously for 2 minutes. Fill 24 greased muffin cups. Bake at 350° for 15 minutes. Remove from pan and cool on wire rack.

Dr. Deb's Advice

In cold weather do not over dress. Many players wear several layers because of the cold weather but this is not a wise decision. Once players start moving around they will get warm due to the fact that the are moving frequently as well as wearing many layers. Once players stop, however, they cool down quickly and their damp clothes saturated by their sweat causes them to become even colder. This mistake usually results in several illnesses.

Championship Chicken and Dumplings

4 or 5 chicken pieces or whole chicken
1 teaspoon salt
1/4 teaspoon pepper
1/8 teaspoon poultry seasoning
1 tablespoon butter
1 carrot, chopped
1 celery stalk, chopped
1 can chicken broth
1 can cream of chicken soup
1 1/2 cans water
3 to 4 cans refrigerated biscuits, torn

Place chicken, salt, pepper, poultry seasoning, butter, carrot and celery in a large kettle. Cover with water and stew about 30 minutes for pieces, longer for whole chicken, until tender. Remove chicken from broth and strain, if desired. Add chicken broth, cream of chicken soup and water. Season to taste. Bring to a low boil and drop torn biscuits into broth. Gently press dumplings down to cover with broth. Cover and simmer about 8 or 10 minutes. Serve with chicken separate or tear chicken into dumplings. Use big bowls.

For extra hungry soccer players, you can add more dumplings in heated broth.

You can stew chicken early in day and just heat up to make dumplings after the game.

Muddy Clete Cake

Two 8-ounce packages cream cheese
2 cups powdered sugar
16 ounces whipped topping
2 small packages instant vanilla pudding mix
4 cups milk
16-ounce package Oreo cookies, crushed

Mix cream cheese and powdered sugar together; blend in whipped topping and mix well. In separate bowl, prepare pudding according to package directions. Layer cookies, then pudding, then whipped topping mixture, ending with cookies on top. It is fun to serve this in an old container that resembles a flower pot or bucket and arrange artificial flowers to stand in it.

Serves 6 to 8

Slidetackling Pepper Steak

1 1/2 pounds round steak
2 tablespoons olive oil
1 envelope onion soup mix
2 cups water
2 medium or 1 large green pepper,
   cut into strips
1 1/2 tablespoons corn starch
1/2 cup water

Cut meat into thin strips 2-inches long. In a large skillet brown meat in olive oil, turning frequently. Stir in onion soup and water. Cover and simmer 30 minutes or until meat is tender. Add green pepper. Blend corn starch with water and stir into skillet until thickened. Serve with rice or noodles.

Serves 4 to 6

Sidekick Sloppy Joes

1 1/2 pounds ground beef
1/2 cup finely chopped onion
1 tablespoon packed brown sugar
1 tablespoon vinegar
2 teaspoons dry mustard
2 tablespoons water
1/2 cup unsalted catsup
8 hamburger buns

Brown ground beef and onion together. Pour off fat. Add brown sugar, vinegar, mustard, water and catsup. Simmer over low heat for 5 minutes or until warm. Serve over hamburger buns which have been split open and toasted.

Makes 8 servings

Goalie's Goulash

1 pound ground beef
1 can baked beans
1 small onion, chopped
1 package egg noodles

In large skillet, brown meat; drain. Add beans and onion. Cook over low heat until hot. Cook noodles according to package directions and combine.

Serves 4

Dr. Deb's Advice

In choosing pregame meals try to choose foods that are low in fats. Fatty foods tend to stay in the stomach longer than those of high protein and carbohydrates. Foods with artificial flavors as well as acids can also upset the stomach during physical activity.

The Captain's Corn Bread

3 slices crisp bacon, crumbled
8 1/2-ounce package corn muffin mix
1 egg
1/4 cup milk
4-ounce can diced green chilies, well drained

Heat oven to 400°. Grease 8x8-inch square pan. In medium bowl, combine all ingredients; mix just until dry ingredients are moistened. Spread into prepared pan. Bake for 15 to 20 minutes or until golden brown.

Makes 9 servings

German Team's Favorite Sausage Dish

One 12 to 16-ounce package knockwurst
2 tablespoons salad oil
1 large red pepper,
    seeded and cut in 1-inch squares
1 large green pepper,
    seeded and cut in 1-inch squares
1 small onion, thinly sliced
Two 16-ounce cans black-eyed peas, drained
Two 6-ounce cans spicy tomato juice

Slice each knockwurst into 3 diagonal pieces. Heat oil in large skillet; sautè knockwurst, pepper squares and onion until vegetables are tender, about 5 minutes. Add peas and tomato juices; stir to combine. Simmer, covered, 10 minutes.

Makes 4 servings

FIFA Fudge Pie

2 sticks butter
4 cups sugar
1 cup cocoa
2 tablespoons flour
6 eggs
2 tablespoons vanilla
1 large can pet milk
2 deep-dish pie shells

Melt butter; mix in sugar, cocoa and flour. Beat eggs and stir in vanilla; pour into cocoa mixture. Beat in pet milk. Pour into pie shells; bake at 350° for 40 minutes. Middle will be shaky but will set up.

Champion Cheese Stuffed Chicken Breasts

1 envelope lemon and herb dry soup mix
1/2 cup plain dry bread crumbs
6 boneless, skinless chicken breast strips
6 ounces sliced mozzarella cheese
3 tablespoons margarine, melted

Preheat oven to 350°. In medium bowl, combine soup mix and bread crumbs. Pound chicken with meat mallet until 1/4-inch thick. Place a slice of cheese in center of chicken breast strip. Roll chicken around cheese and secure with toothpicks. Dip chicken breasts into margarine, then in soup mixture, until evenly coated. Arrange chicken in baking dish. Drizzle with remaining margarine. Bake uncovered until chicken is done. Remove toothpicks before serving.

Players' Potato Soup

6 medium potatoes, peeled and sliced
2 carrots, diced
2 quarts water
1 onion, chopped
6 tablespoons butter
6 tablespoons flour
1 1/2 cups milk
1 teaspoon salt
1/2 teaspoon pepper

Cook potatoes and carrots in water until tender; drain, reserving 1 quart of water. Sautè onion in butter in Dutch oven. Stir in flour; gradually add milk. Cook on low until thickened. Stir in potatoes and carrots; add salt and pepper. Add enough water to make right consistency.

Serves 8

Halftime Ham Casserole

1 box macaroni and cheese
2 cups ham or turkey
1 cup sour cream
10-ounce can of peas and carrots, drained
3/4 cup chopped onion

Cook macaroni and cheese according to package directions. Stir in remaining ingredients. Bake in 325° oven for 20 minutes or until heated through.

Dr. Deb's Advice

While coming out of practice on a cold day players are usually sweating and very warm. Cool down gradually to prevent any sickness.

Kickin' Chicken Fajitas

1 pound chicken tenders
1 tablespoon cooking oil
1/2 cup onion, chopped
1/2 cup green pepper, chopped
1 can diced tomatoes with chili peppers
1/4 teaspoon garlic salt
Dash of cayenne pepper
Dash of cumin
Tortillas
Shredded cheese

Boil chicken in salted water until tender; approximately 20 minutes. Drain and shred or cut into small pieces. Heat oil in skillet and cook onion and pepper until tender. Add chicken, tomatoes and spices. Stir together all ingredients until hot. Spoon into tortillas; sprinkle on cheese and roll.

Pregame Broccoli et Poulè

4 to 6 chicken breasts
2 tablespoons olive oil
1 can mushrooms
1 package frozen broccoli
1 can chicken broth
2 cups instant rice

Brown chicken in hot skillet with olive oil. Drain oil; add mushrooms and simmer 5 minutes. Push chicken to outer part of skillet, leaving a hole in the middle of pan. Add broccoli to the center and pour chicken broth over; cover. Cook over high heat until boiling. Add rice and remove from heat for approximately 6 to 7 minutes.

Backpass Bean and Pasta Soup

1 1/2 pounds low-fat ground beef
Vegetable cooking spray
Three 13 3/4-ounce cans
    fat-free beef broth
Two 5 1/2-ounce cans tomato-vegetable juice
28-ounce can crushed tomatoes
6-ounce can tomato paste
1 1/2 cups chopped onion
1 1/2 cups chopped celery, with leaves
1 1/2 cups shredded carrot
15-ounce can kidney beans,
    drained and rinsed
15-ounce can Northern beans,
    drained and rinsed
1/4 cup lemon juice
1 1/2 teaspoons minced garlic
2 teaspoons dried Italian seasoning
1 1/2 teaspoons ground red pepper
1/2 teaspoon salt
Wagon-wheel pasta,
    cooked without salt or fat

Brown ground beef in large Dutch oven coated with cooking spray, stirring until it crumbles. Drain and pat dry with paper towels. Return to pan and add broth and remaining ingredients except pasta. Bring to a boil; reduce heat and simmer uncovered 45 minutes. Remove from heat and cool. Place desired amount of soup into airtight containers; freeze up to 6 months. When ready to serve thaw soup in refrigerator overnight. Cook over medium heat until thoroughly heated. Stir in 2/3 cup cooked pasta per 3 cups soup mixture.

Re-Kick Romano and Noodles

1/4 cup butter or margarine, softened
2 tablespoons dried parsley flakes
1 teaspoon dried basil, crushed
8-ounce package cream cheese, softened
1/8 teaspoon pepper
2/3 cup boiling water
8 ounces fettuccini, thin noodles
   or spaghetti noodles
1 clove garlic, minced
1/4 cup butter or margarine
3/4 cup shredded or grated Romano
   or Parmesan cheese

Combine butter, parsley flakes and basil; blend in cream cheese and pepper. Stir in boiling water; blend mixture well. Keep warm over pan of hot water. Cook noodles in large amount of boiling salt water until just tender; drain. Cook garlic in butter or margarine, 1 to 2 minutes. Pour over noodles; toss lightly and quickly to coat well. Sprinkle with 1/2 cup of grated cheese; toss again. Pile noodles on warm serving platter; spoon warm cream cheese mixture over. Sprinkle with remaining 1/4 cup grated cheese; garnish with additional parsley.

Serves 6

Referee Wraps

1 package bacon
1 package Little Smokies Sausages
1/2 cup brown sugar

Cut bacon into halves. Wrap around the sausages. Bake at 450° for 15 minutes. Remove from oven, sprinkle with brown sugar and bake for another 15 minutes. Serve warm.

High Five Layered Casserole

2 pounds lean ground beef
1 can golden mushroom soup
1 package dry onion soup mix
1 package mild cheddar cheese, shredded
1 package tater tots

Break uncooked ground beef into pieces and place in 9x9-inch baking dish. Spread mushroom soup over meat; sprinkle with onion soup mix, then cheddar cheese. Place tater tops on cheddar cheese layer. Bake at 350° for 1 hour.

Hat Trick Hamburger Dish

1 pound ground beef
1 small onion, chopped
1 cup cooked macaroni
1 1/2 cups canned tomatoes
1 can chili-beef soup
4 slices American cheese

Cook beef and onion until brown; drain. Add macaroni, tomatoes and soup. Bring to a boil. Lay cheese
on top. Do not stir. Ready to serve when cheese
melts.

Dr. Deb's Advice

Rice and potatoes are an excellent source of energy.

Maradona's White Bean Soup

4 thick-cut slices bacon, chopped
1 medium onion, chopped
1/2 medium cabbage head,
    thinly sliced crosswise
1/8 teaspoon dried red pepper flakes
One and one-half 14 1/2-ounce cans
    chicken broth
Two 15-ounce cans cannellini, Great Northern
    or navy beans, drained and rinsed
1/2 teaspoon ground or rubbed sage
Salt and freshly ground pepper
Minced fresh parsley

Cook bacon in heavy medium saucepan until crisp. Transfer bacon to paper towels using slotted spoon. Reserve half of bacon for garnishing soup. Add onion to pan and cook over medium heat until translucent, stirring occasionally, about 10 minutes. Add cabbage to saucepan and cook until tender, stirring frequently, about 8 minutes. Mix in red pepper flakes, then broth. Stir in beans and sage. Simmer 15 minutes, stirring occasionally. Season with salt and pepper. Can be prepared up to 2 days ahead. Cover and refrigerate. Rewarm over medium-low heat, stirring frequently and thinning with additional broth if necessary. Sprinkle with bacon and parsley.

Winning Season Turkey Wedges

2 cans chunk turkey, drained
1 cup grated Colby-Monterey Jack cheese
3 green onions, chopped
Four soft 10-inch tortillas
Salsa
Sour Cream

Mix turkey, cheese and onions together. Divide between two tortillas. Top with remaining tortillas. Brown in ungreased skillet until crispy. Cut each tortilla into four pieces. Top with salsa and sour cream.

Quick and easy.

End of Game Enchilada Casserole

16-ounce can tamales
16-ounce can chili with no beans
1 medium onion, sliced very thin
2 cups corn chips, broken
6 ounces mild cheddar cheese, sliced

Unwrap tamales; cut into 1/2-inch slices. Line 1 1/2-quart casserole with half the tamale slices. Spread half the chili, half the onions, half the chips and half the cheese over tamale slices. Repeat layers, except for the cheese. Bake, covered at 350° for 25 minutes. Top with remaining cheese slices and bake, uncovered, for 10 more minutes. Serve with sour cream and sliced olives.

Soccer Pete's Pepperoni Bites

1 cup shredded mozzarella cheese
1/2 cup chopped pepperoni
1/2 cup pizza sauce
2 cans of biscuits
1 tablespoon milk
1/4 cup Parmesan cheese

Combine cheese, pepperoni and sauce in a bowl and set aside. Separate biscuits and flatten to 3-inch circles. Place 1 rounded tablespoon of meat mixture in the center. Bring edges of dough together; pinch to seal. Place seam side down on a greased cookie sheet. Brush with milk and sprinkle with Parmesan cheese. Bake in 350° oven for 12 to 15 minutes or until brown.

Makes 20

Upper V
Veggie and Ham Casserole

2 cans mixed vegetables, drained
1 cup mayonnaise
1 cup shredded cheddar cheese
1 can sliced water chestnuts
1 onion, diced
Two 10 1/2-ounce cans mushroom soup
1 to 2 cups chopped ham
1 package butter crackers
1 stick butter, melted

Combine all ingredients except crackers and butter. Place in casserole dish. Mix crackers and butter and sprinkle over casserole. Bake for 20 minutes at 350°.

Serves 6

Competition
Sausage and Rice Casserole

2 pounds pork sausage
1 cup bell pepper, finely chopped
1 cup onion, chopped
2 1/2 cups celery, coarsely chopped
2 small packages instant chicken noodle soup
4 1/2 cups boiling water
1 cup rice, uncooked
1/2 teaspoon salt
1 cup blanched almonds
1/4 cup butter, melted

Brown sausage, pour off excess fat. Add bell pepper, onion and 1 cup celery to sausage and sautè. In a large pan add soup mix to boiling water, stir in rice, cover and simmer for 20 minutes or until tender. Add sausage mixture and salt, stirring well. Pour into buttered baking dish and sprinkle remaining celery and almonds over the top. Drizzle with melted butter. Bake uncovered at 325° for about 30 minutes.

Soccer Fan Sausage Stew

17-ounce can green peas
1 1/2 pounds smoked sausage,
    sliced in 1/2-inch pieces
10 1/2-ounce can French onion soup
28-ounce can whole tomatoes, undrained
2 cups peeled, cubed potatoes
1/2 teaspoon Worcestershire sauce
1/4 cup flour

Drain peas reserving 1/2 cup of the liquid; set aside. Cook sausage in a Dutch oven until brown. Add next 4 ingredients and the peas; bring to a boil. Simmer, uncovered, until potatoes are tender. Stir reserved liquid into the flour and add to the stew. Cook over medium heat until thick and bubbly.

Champion's Cheese Burst Biscuits

10 1/2-ounce can biscuits
2 1/2 ounces American or cheddar cheese,
   cut into ten 3/4-inch cubes
1 tablespoon milk
1 teaspoon sesame, caraway or poppy seed

Heat oven to 400°. Separate dough into 10 biscuits; partial separate each biscuit into 2 layers. Insert one cheese cube; press edge to seal well. Place on ungreased cookie sheet. Cut a deep X on top; brush with milk and sprinkle with seed. Bake for 10 to 12 minutes.

Coaches' Chicken Casserole

1 chicken, boiled and deboned
1 can cream of chicken soup
8-ounce carton sour cream
1 cup cracker crumbs
3 tablespoons melted butter

Mix chicken and soup; add sour cream. Pour into casserole dish. Sprinkle cracker crumbs on top and pour melted butter over. Bake at 400° for 20 to 25 minutes.

Missed Goal Mexican Casserole

One 8-ounce package of Doritos, crushed
1 pound cooked, diced chicken or turkey
1 medium onion, chopped
   or 1/4 cup dried onion
One 10-1/2-ounce can chicken soup
   plus 1/4 cup water
One 10-1/2-ounce can mushroom soup
   plus 1/4 cup water
One 10-ounce can Ro-Tel tomatoes
1/2 pound cheddar or American cheese

Layer ingredients in a 9x13-inch casserole dish starting with half of the Doritos, then chicken, onions, soups, tomatoes and then cheese. Spread rest of Doritos on top. Bake 350° for 30 minutes.

Scoring Spaghetti Pie

6 ounces spaghetti noodles
2 eggs, beaten
1/4 cup freshly grated Parmesan cheese
2 tablespoons butter
1/3 cup chopped onion
1 cup sour cream
1 pound Italian sausage
6-ounce can tomato paste
1 cup water
4 ounces mozzarella cheese, sliced

Break noodles in half. Cook in boiling salted water until done. Drain. While still warm combine noodles with eggs and Parmesan. Pour into a well greased 10-inch pie plate and pat mixture up and around sides with a spoon. Melt butter, add onion and sautè until limp. Stir in sour cream and spoon over noodles. Remove sausage from casing, crumble and cook in skillet until done; drain. Add tomato paste and water; simmer 10 minutes. Spoon sausage on top of sour cream mixture. Bake at 350° for 25 minutes. Arrange mozzarella on top and return to oven until cheese melts.

This freezes well before making, so make two at a time.

World Cup
Corned Beef and Cabbage

One 3 to 4 pound corned beef brisket
3 tablespoons pickling spice
2 cups water
4 to 6 small red potatoes,
  about 1 1/2 pounds
1 small head of cabbage, cut into wedges
3 carrots, cut into thirds
3/4 cup sour cream
2 tablespoons prepared horseradish

Combine brisket, pickling spice and water in a 6-quart pressure cooker. Cover with lid and seal securely; place pressure control over vent tube. Cook over high heat until control rocks back and forth quickly. Reduce heat until pressure control rocks occasionally; cook 50 minutes. Remove from heat, run cold water over cooker to reduce pressure. Carefully remove heat. Remove corned beef; keep warm. Add potatoes, cabbage and carrots to cooker. Cook as previously directed for 5 minutes. Combine sour cream and horseradish. Arrange potatoes, cabbage and carrots around corned beef. Serve sour cream and horseradish mixture with meal.

Serves 4

Corner Flag
Chuck and Cheddar Casserole

1 pound ground chuck, browned and drained
1 clove garlic, minced
Dash of garlic salt and powder
1 teaspoon salt
Dash of pepper
1 teaspoon sugar
Two 8-ounce cans tomato sauce
1/4 cup green olives, sliced
4 ounces small noodles, cooked and drained
5 green onions, chopped, tops and all
1 cup sour cream
3-ounce package cream cheese
Grated Parmesan cheese
1/2 cup or more grated cheddar cheese

In heavy skillet, mix meat, garlic, garlic salt and powder, salt, pepper, sugar and tomato sauce. Cover and simmer 15 minutes. Add green olives. Mix green onions, sour cream and cream cheese; blend. In lightly greased baking dish layer half the noodles, meat sauce, then sour cream mixture. Top with a shaking of Parmesan. Repeat layers and top all with cheddar cheese. Bake at 350° for about 25 minutes.

Hurry I'm Late Chicken and Rice

4 chicken breasts
1 1/3 cups minute rice
1 1/4 cups boiling water
1 can celery soup
1 package onion soup mix
Salt, pepper, paprika to taste

Brown chicken in cooking oil; set aside. Combine rest of ingredients in 1 1/2-quart casserole dish. Place chicken on top of rice mixture. Cover and bake at 350° for 1 1/2 hours.

Dr. Deb's Advice

Bruises and strains do not heal over night. Warm up and stretch properly even after bruises and strains are no longer seen or felt.

Hawaiian Quesadillas for Champs

Eight 8-inch flour tortillas
8-ounce can pineapple tidbits, drained
5-ounce can chunky chicken in water,
    drained and flaked
8-ounce package Monterey Jack Cheese
1/3 cup sliced green onions
1/4 teaspoon pepper
1 cup chunky salsa
Fresh cilantro

Place 2 tortillas on each sheet, using 2 ungreased baking sheets. Combine pineapple and chicken. Spoon over tortillas. Top each tortilla evenly with cheese, onions and pepper. Top with remaining 4 tortillas. Bake at 350 degrees for 8-10 minutes or until cheese softens. Cut each tortilla into 4 wedges. Spoon 1 tablespoon salsa over each wedge and garnish with cilantro.

Energy Packed Peanut Butter Pie

8 ounces cream cheese
1 cup powdered sugar
1/2 cup smooth peanut butter
8 ounces whipped topping
Graham cracker pie crust

Mix all ingredients except pie crust. Pour into pie crust and garnish with grated chocolate bar or melt a few chocolate chips. Pour drops onto pie. Run a knife through the pie and refrigerate for at least one hour before slicing.

Great pie!

Soccer Sam's Skillet Spaghetti

1 pound ground beef
2 teaspoons chili powder
1 1/2 teaspoons dried oregano, crushed
1 teaspoon sugar
1 teaspoon salt
1 teaspoon garlic salt
One 6-ounce can tomato paste
2 1/4 cups tomato juice
2 tablespoons minced onion
3 1/2 cups water
One 7-ounce package spaghetti noodles,
    uncooked
Grated Parmesan cheese

In 12-inch skillet, brown ground beef; drain off excess fat. Stir in chili powder, oregano, sugar, salt and garlic salt. Blend in tomato paste. Stir in tomato juice, onion and water; bring to a boil. Carefully add noodles; stir to separate strands. Cover and simmer, stirring frequently, for 30 minutes. Serve with grated cheese.

Serves 4 to 6

Hamburger Casserole for the Pros

1 pound ground beef
1 onion, peeled and chopped
6 potatoes, diced
1 can cream of mushroom soup
1/2 cup milk
2 tablespoons butter
1 pound Velveeta

Brown ground beef and onion. Boil potatoes separately. Mix beef, soup, milk, butter, Velveeta and potatoes in a covered casserole dish. Bake at 350° for 20 minutes or until cheese is melted.

Official's Choice Pork Roast with Cherry Sauce

4 to 6 pound pork loin
12 ounces cherry preserves
1/2 cup light corn syrup
1/4 cup red wine vinegar
1/4 teaspoon each: salt, nutmeg,
   cloves and cinnamon
1/8 teaspoon black pepper
1/4 cup slivered, blanched almonds

Bake pork loin, uncovered, at 350° for approximately 3 hours. Bring remaining ingredients except almonds to a boil; boil 1 minute and add almonds. Baste roast several times with sauce during last 30 minutes of cooking. Serve remaining sauce warm with roast.

Dr. Deb's Advice

Being in shape results in less injuries and less cramps, as well as higher endurance and better playing performance.

Gold Medal Chicken Casserole

3 pound chicken, cooked
1 can cream of mushroom soup
1 can cream of celery soup
1 cup chicken broth
1 package stuffing mix
1 stick margarine

Debone chicken and set aside. Mix soups and broth well with a mixer. Melt butter and add stuffing mix. Set aside 1 cup of stuffing mixture. In a 9x13-inch pan layer half each of the chicken, stuffing mixture and soup mixture. Repeat and top with the cup of stuffing set aside. Bake at 350° for 30 minutes or until bubbly and brown.

World Ranking
Beef and Zucchini Pie

2 cups chopped zucchini
2 cups string beans, drained and rinsed
1 cup chopped tomatoes
1/2 cup chopped onions
1 pound ground beef, cooked and drained
3 eggs, well beaten
1/2 teaspoon black pepper
3/4 cup biscuit mix
1 1/2 cups milk
1 cup grated cheese

Heat oven to 350°. Grease 9 1/2x13-inch baking dish. Layer bottom of pan with zucchini; add beans, tomatoes, onions and ground beef. Set aside. Mix eggs, pepper, biscuit mix and milk in blender for about 1 minute. Pour evenly over ingredients. Spread cheese over top of casserole. Bake for 1 hour.

Makes 6 to 8 servings

South of the Border
Mexican Casserole

1 pound ground beef
1 pound can tomatoes
1 pound can kidney beans
1 3/4-ounce envelope chili mix
1 1/2 cups corn chips, broken into pieces
1/2 to 1 cup cheddar cheese, shredded
2 cups lettuce, shredded
1 medium tomato, chopped
1/4 cup ripe olives, pitted

Brown ground beef; drain well. Add tomatoes, kidney beans and chili mix. Spoon into casserole dish. Sprinkle with corn chips and cheese. Bake at 350° for 15 minutes or until cheese melts. Top with lettuce, tomatoes and olives.

Makes 5 to 6 servings

Playoff Chicken Pot Pie

Two pie crusts
2 cans mixed vegetables, drained
Two 10 1/2-ounce cans
   cream of chicken soup
2 cans deboned chicken

Layer one of the crusts in the bottom of an 8x8-inch casserole dish. Mix vegetables, soup and chicken; pour over crust. Top with second crust. Pinch edges and brush with melted butter. Bake at 350° for 40 to 45 minutes.

Dr. Deb's Advice

To lose weight properly select foods low in fat and increase physical activity (at least 45 minutes to one hour a day). Also drink 6 to 8 glasses of water per day. This helps to cleanse and purify the digestive system.

Fastest Ever
Chocolate Chip Cookies

2 sticks margarine
1 1/2 cups brown sugar
2 eggs
1 teaspoon vanilla flavoring
1 teaspoon baking soda
2 1/4 cups self-rising flour
8 ounces chocolate chips

Preheat oven to 350 degrees and place margarine sticks on cookie sheet pan and place in oven to melt. Meanwhile cream sugar and eggs, adding vanilla and soda. Carefully remove pan with butter and pour into egg mixture. Add 1/2 of flour and mix well. Add remaining flour and mix again, then chocolate chips. Spread mixture over 15 1/2 x 10 1/2-inch cookie pan and bake for 10 minutes or until light brown. Cool a few minutes, then cut in squares and serve warm with a big glass of milk!

Corner Kick Chick-Enchiladas

1 cup onion, chopped
1/2 cup green pepper, chopped
2 tablespoons margarine
2 cups chopped, cooked chicken
1 can chopped green chili peppers
3 tablespoons margarine
1/4 cup flour
1 teaspoon coriander
3/4 teaspoon salt
2 1/2 cups chicken broth
1 cup sour cream or plain yogurt
1/2 cup Monterey Jack cheese, grated
Twelve 6-inch tortillas

In a large saucepan, cook onion and green pepper in margarine until tender. Combine in a bowl with chicken and chili peppers. In same saucepan melt margarine. Stir in flour, coriander and salt. Stir in chicken broth and sour cream or yogurt; cook until thick and bubbly. Cook and stir 2 minutes more. Remove from heat. Stir 1/2 cup of sauce in chicken mixture. Dip each tortilla into sauce; fill each with 1/4 cup chicken. Roll up. Arrange in 9x13-inch baking dish. Pour on remaining sauce, sprinkle with grated cheese and bake, uncovered, at 350° for 25 minutes.

Away Game
Chicken and Rice Casserole

4 pounds chicken breasts
2 boxes wild rice
3 to 4 chopped onions
2 sticks butter
3 tablespoons flour
1 1/2 cans mushroom soup
1 cup milk
1 large can sliced mushrooms
Salt and pepper to taste
1 pound sharp cheese, grated

Cook and debone chicken. Cook rice. Sautè onions in butter; add flour, soup and milk. Add mushrooms and seasonings. Alternate layers of rice, chicken and mushroom filling. Cover top with cheese. Bake at 325° for 20 to 30 minutes.

Makes 20 servings

Futbol Chicken Fiesta

One 16-ounce package frozen broccoli
1 box chicken flavored stuffing
8 ounces Velveeta cheese, cubed
One 14 1/2-ounce can cream of chicken soup
2 cups cooked chicken, cut in small pieces

Cook broccoli; drain well. Prepare stuffing according to package directions. Heat together cubed cheese and soup, stirring until cheese melts. Layer broccoli in 2 1/2-quart casserole dish. Add chicken; pour soup mixture over chicken. Put prepared stuffing on top. Cover. Bake at 350° for 30 minutes.

Smushroom Soup

3/4 cup chopped onions
2 cups sliced mushrooms
3 tablespoons melted butter
2 tablespoons flour
2 cups milk
1 cup water
2 to 3 chicken bouillon cubes
Milk

Sautè onions and mushrooms in butter; stir in flour. Gradually add milk and water, stirring well. Add bouillon cubes; simmer over low heat until dissolved. Pour mixture into large soup kettle and add milk until desired consistency is reached. Simmer over low heat for one hour.

The Top Player's Taco Casserole

1 1/2 pounds ground beef
1 onion, finely chopped
1 can tomato bits
1/2 can water
1 package taco seasoning
1 can chili beans
1 package Dorito chips with cheese
1 can chopped green chilies
8 ounces sour cream
8 ounces grated cheddar cheese

Brown ground beef and onion; drain. Combine tomato bits, water, taco seasoning and chili beans to hamburger mixture. In casserole dish layer the following: half of the Dorito chips, a third of the hamburger mixture, half of the sour cream and half of the green chilies. Repeat the layers. Add last third of the hamburger mixture and top with grated cheddar cheese. Bake at 350° for 30 minutes.

I usually add extra tomato bits and taco seasoning to my casserole.

The Challenger's
Easy Chicken and Dumplings

Two 10 1/2-ounce cans
    cream of chicken soup
2 cans of water
1 cup cooked chicken
6 soft tortilla shells

Heat soup and water until smooth. Add chicken.
Tear tortilla shells in pieces and drop into soup.
Cover pan; cook until tortilla pieces are soft and
fluffy.

The Bleacher Bum's Beef Burgundy

1 1/2 pounds sirloin, cubed
1 can onion soup
1 cup burgundy
1/4 cup bread crumbs
1 bay leaf
1/2 teaspoon rosemary

Cook all ingredients 5 or 6 hours in crock pot. Serve over rice or noodles.

Dr. Deb's Advice

If a muscle strain occurs certain precautions must be taken. Immediately after the strain occurs keep strained area warm and covered by a layer of clothing such as thin shorts, bicycle shorts, or spandex. Double your warm up time to ensure that the affected area is properly stretched. After games and practices be sure to ice down the strained area.

Breakaway Bread Pudding

2 cups dry bread cubes
4 cups milk, scalded
1 tablespoon butter
1/4 teaspoon salt
3/4 cup sugar
4 eggs, slightly beaten
1 teaspoon vanilla
1/2 cup raisins

Soak bread in milk for 5 minutes. Add butter, salt and sugar. Pour slowly over eggs; add vanilla and mix. Put into greased baking dish. Bake at 350° in pan of hot water until firm, around 50 minutes. Serve warm. Add raisins and top with Lemon Sauce.

(Lemon Sauce recipe on following page)

Lemon Sauce

1/2 cup sugar
1/2 teaspoon salt
1 tablespoon cornstarch
1/8 teaspoon nutmeg
1 cup boiling water
1 1/2 tablespoons lemon juice
2 tablespoons butter

Mix first 4 ingredients; gradually add water. Cook over low heat until thick and clear. Add butter and juice; stir well.

Chicken Salsa Shootout

4 to 6 chicken breasts
1 tablespoon cooking oil
One 16-ounce jar of mild, medium or hot salsa

Spray large skillet with cooking spray. Add tablespoon of oil and brown chicken breasts. Add salsa and heat to a boil. Cover and reduce heat to simmer; turn chicken once. Continue simmering for 15 minutes for boneless or 30 minutes if not.

Midfielder Meatballs

1 beaten egg
One 10 3/4-ounce can
    condensed tomato soup
1/4 cup long grain rice
2 tablespoons finely chopped onion
1 tablespoon snipped parsley
1/2 teaspoon salt
1/8 teaspoon pepper
1 pound ground beef
1 tablespoon Worcestershire sauce

In a bowl combine egg and 1/4 cup of soup. Stir in uncooked rice, onion, parsley, salt and pepper. Add beef and mix well. Shape meat into 20 small balls; place in a 10-inch skillet. Mix remaining soup with Worcestershire sauce and 1/2 cup water; pour over meatballs. Bring to a boil; reduce heat. Cover and simmer 35 to 40 minutes, stirring often. Serve with noodles.

Makes 4 to 5 servings

Gameday Garlic Wedges

10-ounce can refrigerated pizza crust
2 tablespoons oil
3 teaspoons dried parsley flakes
3 teaspoons prepared, chopped garlic
1/8 teaspoon coarsely ground black pepper

Heat oven to 425°. Grease 12-inch pizza pan or 9x13-inch pan. Unroll dough and place in pan; starting at center, press out with hands. In small bowl, combine remaining ingredients. Brush over pizza crust. Bake for 13 to 18 minutes or until crust is deep golden brown. Cut into 8 wedges. Serve warm.

The Kicker's Crock Pot BBQ Turkey Breast

1 medium turkey breast
One 16-ounce bottle barbecue sauce

Spray crock pot with cooking spray. Place turkey breast in crock pot; cover with barbecue sauce. Heat on high for 4 to 6 hours or on low for 8 to 10 hours. Serve with salad, vegetable and bread.

Serves 4

Speedy Little Devils

One devils food cake mix
1 stick butter or margarine, melted
1/2 cup of creamy peanut butter
7 or 7 1/2-ounce jar marshmallow creme

Combine dry cake mix and butter or margarine; reserve 1 1/2 cups for the top crust. Put remaining crumb mixture into ungreased 9x13x2-inch pan. Top with combined peanut butter and marshmallow creme; spread evenly. Crumble remaining mixture on top. Bake 20 minutes at 350°. Cool before slicing.

Yellow Card Crock Pot Chicken

1 chicken, whole or cut up
2 carrots, sliced
1 onion, sliced
2 celery stalks, chopped
2 teaspoons salt
1/2 teaspoon pepper
1/2 cup chicken broth
1/2 teaspoon basil

Put chicken, carrots, onions and celery in bottom of a crock pot. Top with salt, pepper and broth. Sprinkle basil on top. Cover and cook on low for 8 to 10 hours or on high for 2 1/2 to 3 1/2 hours.

Dr. Deb's Advice

If you are insistent on eating any type of meat as a pregame meal be sure to bake meat instead of frying.

Striker Scotchies

2 cups flour
2 teaspoons baking powder
1 teaspoon baking soda
1 teaspoon salt
1 cup butter, softened
1 1/2 cups brown sugar
2 eggs
1 tablespoon water
One 12-ounce package butterscotch morsels
1 1/2 cups dry oatmeal
1/2 teaspoon orange extract

Combine flour, baking powder, baking soda and salt; set aside. Cream butter, brown sugar, eggs and water. Gradually add flour mixture. Stir in morsels, oatmeal and orange extract. Drop by tablespoons onto cookie sheets. Bake at 375° for 10 to 12 minutes. Cool on rack.

Makes 48 cookies

Last Minute Lasagna

1 pound lean ground chuck
1 cup chopped onion
3 cloves garlic, finely chopped
4 cups tomato juice
8 ounces mushrooms, optional
1 can tomato paste
1 teaspoon oregano leaves
1 teaspoon parsley flakes
1/2 teaspoon salt
1/8 teaspoon pepper
8 ounces lasagna noodles, uncooked
16 ounces small curd cottage cheese
1 1/2 cups grated Parmesan cheese
2 cups shredded Mozzarella cheese
Parsley flakes

Preheat oven to 350°. Brown meat in large saucepan; add onion and garlic; drain off fat. Stir in tomato juice, mushrooms, tomato paste and seasonings. Simmer 30 minutes, stirring occasionally. In a 9x13-inch baking dish, layer 1/2 each of the uncooked noodles, sauce and three cheeses. Repeat layering; top with parsley. Cover with aluminum foil and bake 30 minutes. Remove foil; continue baking, uncovered, an additional 15 minutes. Remove from oven and let stand 20 minutes before cutting.

Serves 6 to 8.

Note: lasagna can be prepared ahead and refrigerated. Bake, covered, 45 minutes; uncover and continue baking 15 minutes.

Loose Clete
Cheeseburger Casserole

1 to 1 1/2 pounds ground beef
Spaghetti sauce
4 to 6 slices cheese
1 can biscuits

Brown meat and drain; stir in spaghetti sauce. Pat meat mixture in bottom of casserole dish. Lay cheese all over top and put biscuits on top of cheese. Bake according to directions for making biscuits on label.

Serves 4 to 6

Instep Italian Chicken

4 to 6 chicken breasts
One 16-ounce jar primavera spaghetti sauce
2 ounces each: mozzarella,
   Colby and Monterey Jack cheese
Grated Parmesan cheese

Preheat oven to 400°. Spray large casserole dish with cooking spray. Add chicken breasts and bake for 15 minutes. Turn chicken and add spaghetti sauce. Top the sauce with mozzarella, Colby and Monterey Jack cheeses in layers on the chicken breasts. Bake an additional 15 minutes or until chicken is tender and cheese has melted. Sprinkle grated Parmesan on chicken pieces and serve with rice or pasta.

In Your Pocket Oatmeal Treat

1/2 cup honey
1/2 cup peanut butter
1 cup nonfat dry milk powder
1 cup rolled oats or crushed cereal

Measure and stir all ingredients together. Roll about one spoonful in hands to make a ball. Place on waxed paper to dry a little. Store in a flat container wrapped air tight.

Juggling Nacho Jumble

1 1/2 pounds ground beef
1 medium onion, diced
1 bell pepper, diced
1 bag tortilla chips
1 package shredded cheddar cheese
Shredded lettuce
2 tomatoes, diced
Taco sauce

Brown meat, onions and green pepper; drain off fat. Crush chips into bottom of 9x13-inch pan. Spread with half the meat mixture. Add a layer of cheese; remaining meat mixture and another layer of cheese. Bake at 350° until cheese is melted and brown. May add taco sauce. Add lettuce and tomatoes to top.

Serves 4

Soccer Terms

Back pass: also known as a drop, a back pass is when a player passes the ball to a person directly behind them.

Break away: an occurrence in which a player has advanced past the opposing team's forward, midfield and defensive line to put himself in a one on one encounter with the opposing team's goalkeeper.

Captain: player on a team chosen to be the leader of the team.

Center circle: a circle in the middle of the field with a diameter of ten yards that is the starting point for all soccer games.

Cleats: studded soccer shoes worn by soccer players to gain better traction while playing.

Corner flag: flags that stand in the four corners of the soccer field to mark the out of bounds as well as to give the referee an idea of when the ball has gone out of bounds.

Corner kick: in an occurrence in which the ball has crossed the goal line to go out of bounds and was last touched by the defending team a corner kick will be awarded to the attacking team. The ball is placed in a designated spot in one of the two corners and then kicked into play.

Crossbar: the top beam on a goal connecting the two posts.

Defense: also known as fullbacks, these players objectives are to keep the other team from getting in scoring position.

FIFA: Federal International Futbol Association. In charge of organizing the World Cups as well as various other tournaments. FIFA is also in charge of approving the production of soccer products such as shin guards, balls, cleats and goals. FIFA also determines the size of lines, goal areas, arcs and all other dimensions for soccer fields.

Forwards: first line of an attacking soccer team whose main objective is to score.

Fullbacks: also known as the defense, full backs main objective is to keep the opposing team out of scoring position.

Free kick: situation in which play is stopped for a foul or by referee's own choice and restarted by placing the ball on the spot where it was when the whistle was blown. The team who committed the foul will then back up 10 yards from the designated spot while the opposing team kicks it into play. There are indirect free kicks in which the ball has to touch another player before being in play and there are direct free kicks in which the ball is in play as soon as it is kicked.

Futbol: Spanish for soccer.

Halfbacks: also known as midfielders the main objective of these players is to put the ball in scoring position as well as assisting the forwards in their efforts to score.

Half volley: occurrence in which a player kicks the ball a split second after it has bounced off the ground causing the ball's momentum to shift, sending it a greater distance at a greater speed.

Handball: offense committed when a player, who is not the goalie, strikes the ball with his hand.

Hat trick: when a player scores three goals in a game.

Instep kick: when a player leans over the ball

while kicking it so that the ball will stay at a lower height.

Juggling: to keep the ball in the air using only your legs, feet, chest and head.

Keeper: also known as the goalie this player can use his/her hands to stop the ball from entering the goal.

Kickoff: the starting of a soccer game.

Linesman: a referee whose job is to run up and down the sidelines assisting the center referee with fouls, out of bounds and off sides.

Maradona: Diego Maradona is a world famous soccer player who plays for Argentina national team.

Pele: a world famous soccer icon who played for Brazil.

Penalty kick: if a foul or offense is committed within the 18 yard goal box then in some cases a penalty kick will be awarded to the attacking team. All players with the exception of the player who is kicking and the goalie who is defending the goal are supposed to stand outside the 18 yard box. A shot from a designated spot about 6 paces from the goal.

PK: another term for penalty kick.

Post: the two side beams of a goal that support the crossbar.

Red card: card given to a player after being charged with a foul or offense. The result is suspension from the present game as well as the following game.

Re-kick: if a free kick is taken too soon or not from the right spot then a re-kick will be issued and the kick will be taken over.

Save: occurrence in which the goalkeeper stops the ball from entering the goal.

Shoot out: in the event of a tie after two overtimes and two halves of sudden death a shoot out will be held. Both teams will then select 5 players who were on the field at the end of sudden death to take shots in the shoot out. Each player will then take one shot from the PK mark against the opposing team's keeper. All other players beside these two players must be outside of the 18 yard area. Both teams alternate shooting and after the last player has kicked, the team with the most goals wins.

Slide tackle: situation in which a player slides feet first at the feet of an opposing player in attempt to take the ball.

Striker: another term used for forwards.

Sudden death: if the score is tied after two overtimes then two sudden death halves will be played. The first team to score during sudden death wins the match.

Upper V: the top two corners of a goal.

World Cup: international soccer tournament that takes place every four years and is considered the most important event in soccer.

Yellow card: is a warning given to a player charged for a foul or offense. Two yellow cards equal one red card.

A special thanks to these Lyon County, Kentucky soccer moms for their recipes.

Jill Akridge
Lynn M. Aldridge
Frances Baccus
Patti Baker
Cindy Bates
Jeannie Bryant
Tina Childress
Drew Coomer
Rhonda Cowan
Paula Cunningham
Marcia Daniel
Nancye Daniel
Sandy Flick

Lynne Fralick
Evan Gilland
Grant Gilland
Vickie Gilland
Patty Gonnella
Lee Ann Goodson
Melody Gray
Carol Gregory
Kathy Gresham
Brenda Knoth
Margaret Kyle
Margaret McQuigg
Shanda Melton
Barbara Meredith
Collin Murphy
Megan Murphy
Pam Norman

Byron Palmiter
Mandy Palmiter
Ron Palmiter
Ruth Palmiter
Pam Pierce
Linda Rehberg
Teresa Ritter
Nancy Staton
Marilyn Terry
Pam Timmons
Judy Travis
Martha Wadlington
Ann Walker
Cheryl Walker
Anne Webber
Cindy Yandell

Index

Soccer Mom Cookbook   Mail to: McClanahan Publishing House, Inc.
P. O. Box 100
Kuttawa, KY 42055

For Orders call TOLL FREE 1-800-544-6959
Visa & MasterCard accepted

Please send me _____ copies of

Soccer Mom Cookbook   @ $ 10.95 each   _____
     Postage & handling   3.50
Kentucky residents add 6% sales tax   @.65 each   _____

Total enclosed   _____

Make check payable to McClanahan Publishing House

Ship to:
NAME _____

ADDRESS _____

CITY _____ STATE _____ ZIP _____

For your team's fund raising activities please contact McClanahan Publishing House, Inc. for ordering and price information on *Soccer Mom Cookbook.*